# HE WAS ONE OF US

RIEN POORTVLIET

# HE WAS ONE OF US

Text by Hans Bouma
Translated by Brian McDermott

BANTAM BOOKS
TORONTO · NEW YORK · LONDON

HE WAS ONE OF US:
The Life of Jesus of Nazareth

A Bantam Book/published by arrangement with
Doubleday & Company, Inc.

PRINTING HISTORY

This book was originally published in Dutch under the
title HIJ WAS EEN VAN ONS by Unieboek BV — Van Holkema
& Warendorf, Bussum and Semper Agendo, BV, Apeldoorn.

Doubleday edition published November 1978

A condensed version appeared in the Christian Herald, Spring 1978

Bantam edition/November 1979

ISBN 0-553-01184-7

Published simultaneously in the United States and Canada

---

Bantam Books are published by Bantam Books, Inc.
Its trademark, consisting of the words "Bantam Books"
and the portrayal of a bantam, is Registered in
U.S. Patent and Trademark Office and in other countries.
Marca Registrada. Bantam Books, Inc.,
666 Fifth Avenue, New York, New York 10019.

---

PRINTED IN THE UNITED STATES OF AMERICA
0 9 8 7 6 5 4 3 2 1

It wasn't my intention in this book to try to sketch how Mary, Peter or Barabbas looked; and certainly not Jesus' face as it might have been.

But, because the familiar Bible texts can sound much too familiar to us—while for others they are incomprehensible—I have tried to tell the story of Jesus by letting faces and hands do the talking. Because faces and hands speak their own language and so they can express more clearly the fact that the people who lived when Jesus was on the earth were completely ordinary folk. There was nothing of the saint about them. They weren't any different than we and we can recognize their outward behavior right off, each of us is Peter and Thomas and Judas and the innkeeper, who, sorry though he was, had no room...

If, while looking at the pictures, you are not able to discover what is going on, you should reach for your Bible. The story of Jesus is found in the Gospels of Matthew, Mark, Luke and John.

I'm very happy that Hans Bouma has written texts for the various pictures.

## He does what nobody does

What is it that is characteristic about Jesus? It is tempting to pin down in his divinity. That way you can keep some distance. He's got to remain a bit of a stranger. The more divine, the less dangerous. All too human is risky business. And it makes sense, doesn't it? It's not for nothing is it, that Jesus is called "Son of God"?

Of course, but not ahead of time. He gets this title only later. He first has to become it. It isn't that easy. It's the man Jesus with whom the Gospels are so taken. On that basis he becomes head of humanity. He lives as one completely original, authentic, consistent. He does what nobody does. He is the Just One. He knows what love is. He shares himself until the very end. He is a heartwarming brother, an indefatigable friend. Jesus is the man in whom God so ardently hoped. He didn't simply come out of the blue. Jesus answered people's expectation. God recognizes himself in him; he can find himself totally in him. Jesus is a great relief for God. At long last a man who is in his image and likeness without fail. Finally someone who fully lives in the Spirit. Jesus is truly a man of God. Or should we say: a Son of the Father? He has a right to that title. Little by little, he seems indeed to be the one. It can't be wrong. Whoever lived as he lived, must be "Son of God." The Roman centurion was right when he confessed: "Truly, this was a Son of God." But in order to be able to choose sides with him, we'll need to stand, like him, next to the cross, where Jesus experiences his humanity to the utmost.

That cross brings us up short right away at what is impossible about Jesus' humanity. He doesn't save it. In this world— inhuman through and through—he had to run amuck. He is irritating; he calls forth resistance. He unmasks us. What remains of us over against him, the truly human one? We hopelessly own who we are. This Jesus accuses us. He is an upstart, a spell-breaker. Isn't he a traitor, a danger for society? Wouldn't it be better if he disappeared?

This book can be looked upon as an act of homage to Jesus' humanity. But this does not mean that the man Jesus is pictured on every page. It is much more people around him that you'll get to see. Ordinary folk who uniquely characterize Jesus in his humanity through their genuinely human reactions to all that Jesus does. Rien Poortvliet is fascinated by everything that Jesus sets in motion. Looking at the people in this book, you know who Jesus is.

What kind of real, human reactions do we meet in this book? Reactions of surprise, wonderment, delight, devotion, but in addition to that—and especially—alienation, bewilderment, mockery, rejection, aggressiveness, hate.

He was one of us. He is the only truly human one who has "survived." But he doesn't leave us out in the cold. He is so much one of us that he is one with us. As far as he is concerned, his humanity is our humanity. He is only happy when we have taken over his way of being, so that we too, as "sons and daughters of God," finally will appear: men and women as we are called to be.

Hans Bouma

AN ORDINARY GIRL
NOTHING STRIKING ABOUT HER

SHE'LL BE GETTING MARRIED

THE MOTHER OF JESUS

SHE IS ORDINARY

ENOUGH FOR THAT

MARY HIS BELOVED
SO STRANGE, SO DISTANT

WHAT SHOULD HE DO
ISN'T HE TOO MUCH

TO REMAIN HERS
TO MARRY HER

SHARE IN HER SECRET
EVEN THIS SECRET

SUDDENLY A CHILD
AND WHAT A CHILD

AND THEN EVEN MORE
HEAVY TAXATION
ON THEIR LAND IN BETHLEHEM

ROMAN OFFICIALS
MAP IT OUT
AND DETERMINE THE ASSESSMENT

THEY HAVE TO BE THERE
THAT MIGHT MAKE A DIFFERENCE

IN NO TIME MARY WILL BE DUE

BUT THEY START ON THEIR WAY

TWO PEOPLE
WHO GET NOTHING
HANDED TO THEM

NOT SEEING HIM
YOU BRING WHAT YOU CAN INTO THE HOUSE
IT'S ALREADY CROWDED ENOUGH

HE'S SORRY
IF THEY HAD BEEN A BIT EARLIER
PERHAPS ELSEWHERE . . .

THAT'S HOW IT STARTED
FACES AJAR
DOORS QUICKLY SHUT AGAIN

CLOSED
    TIGHTLY SHUT HEARTS

SO IT IS ALWAYS
        INCONVENIENT
A THOUSAND EXCUSES

THAT'S HOW IT WILL END

NO ROOM
  WITH PEOPLE
YOUR FAMILY
OWES YOU IT

THANK GOD
THE ANIMALS
ARE THERE TOO

JESUS SHALL
NEVER FORGET IT

NOT FOR THEM
DESPISED OUTCASTS
THEY DIDN'T COUNT

NOT FOR THEM ?
FOR WHOM ELSE

PEACE ON EARTH
JUSTICE FOR THE OPPRESSED

THE LORD WHO SEEKS
WHAT IS LOST

A MAN   A WOMAN
A CHILD

SO HUMAN
SO INESCAPABLE

HERE GOD HOLDS
OPEN HOUSE

HE LETS
HIMSELF BE KNOWN

THE DAY OF THEIR LIVES
FACE TO FACE WITH THE CHILD
IT MAKES THEM YOUNG AGAIN

A LIGHT FOR ISRAEL
A SUN THAT RISES
OVER THE PEOPLES

THEY KNOW ENOUGH
THE PROOF OF GOD'S FIDELITY
LIES IN THEIR HANDS

THE ONE THING LEFT TO THEM
IS TO PRAISE AND GLORIFY

THE WISE MEN FOLLOW A LIGHT
THE SOUGHT AND FOUND
KING OF THEIR DREAMS

COME ON, FORGET IT
IT'S TOO GOOD TO BE TRUE
THIS IS NOT THE FUTURE

THE CHILD MUST DIE
WHAT JUST BEGAN
IS RIGHT AWAY CRUSHED

NO CROWN
A SWORD HANGS OVER
THE CHILD'S HEAD

ANY CHILD
COULD BE JESUS

HEROD
TAKES NO CHANCES

BETHLEHEM DROWNS
IN THE BLOOD

HEROD
CAN RELAX

JESUS IS ALIVE
HE DIED

THE DEATH OF HIS LITTLE
BROTHERS AND SISTERS

JUST WAIT

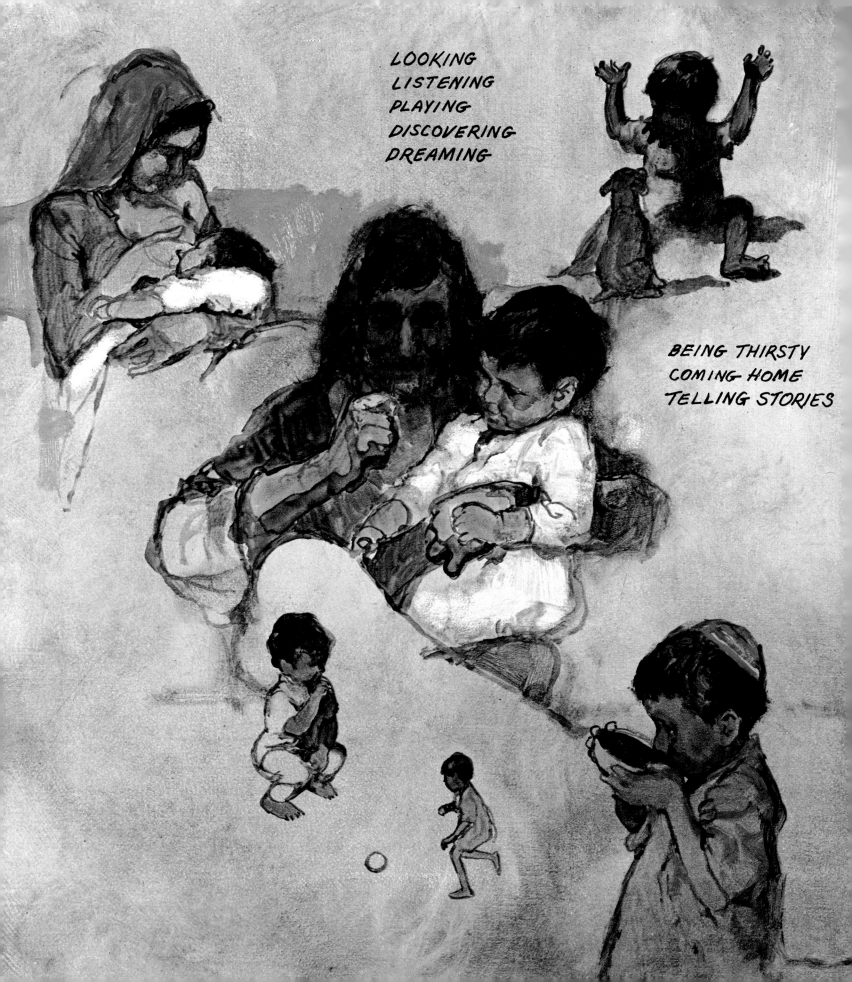

LOOKING
LISTENING
PLAYING
DISCOVERING
DREAMING

BEING THIRSTY
COMING HOME
TELLING STORIES

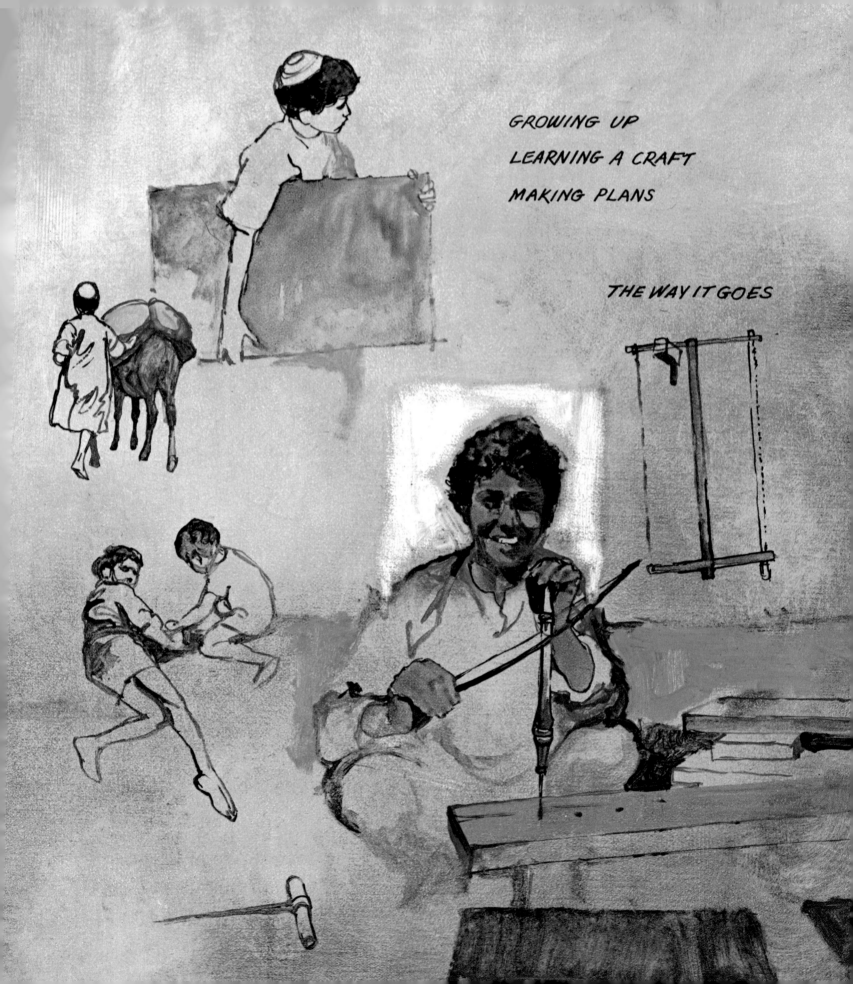

GROWING UP
LEARNING A CRAFT
MAKING PLANS

THE WAY IT GOES

HE ENJOYED THINGS
FORGOT EVERYTHING
JUST ASKED AND TALKED

COMPLETELY IN HIS ELEMENT
A CHILD IN GOD'S HOUSE

AND HIS PARENTS LOOKED
AND LOOKED

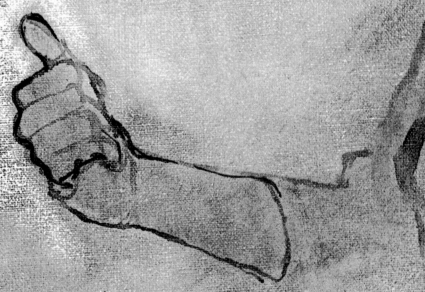

WHAT'S GOT INTO HIM
THEY DON'T KNOW HIM

MARY CALLS HIM UP SHORT
HE SHOULD KNOW HIS PLACE

HE GOES APART, CATCHES HIS BREATH, THE TIME HAS ALMOST COME
ALL ALONE, JUST SOME ANIMALS, JUST HIS GOD

WHAT IS HE SETTING IN MOTION

HIS ENEMY DOESN'T ALLOW HIM REST, BUT TRIES TO CONVERT HIM
HE DOESN'T HUNGER AFTER POWER, HONOR, POSSESSIONS

HE IS PERISHING FROM HUNGER AFTER JUSTICE, HE
YEARNS FOR PEACE
HIS ENEMY KNOWS WHAT HE IS UP TO

YOU HAVE YOUR WORK
YOU'RE BUILDING TOWARD SOMETHING
THERE'S A WOMAN
AND CHILDREN

AND THEN THE VOICE
OF THAT STRANGER
THAT LOOK     THAT GESTURE

WHAT ARE YOU SUPPOSED TO DO
YOU'RE DEFENSELESS
          HE'S THE ONE

THE ONLY THING TO DO IS
TO FOLLOW HIM
COST WHAT IT MIGHT

UNHEARD OF

BEWILDERING     STAGGERING        DANGEROUS
LIBERATING   HEALING   A REVELATION   THE END


THIS CHANGES EVERYTHING


HE SAYS WHAT REALLY MATTERS, NOW YOU KNOW
THIS IS A MAN WHO FULFILLS THE LAW, A JUST ONE



        A MAN OF GOD

HE ATTRACTS IT, HE CAN'T DO ANYTHING AGAINST IT
PAIN, SICKNESS, DEATH — HE HATES IT
HIS GOD HAD SOMETHING ELSE IN MIND

PETER'S MOTHER-IN-LAW KNEW IT

JESUS CAN COUNT ON HIM
HE'S A LIKELY CHAP

DOES HE BELIEVE IT HIMSELF
HE DOESN'T KNOW WHAT HE IS SAYING

JESUS IS DIFFERENT
HE DOES WHAT NOBODY DOES

HE IS THE JUST ONE
WHO CAN HOLD OUT WITH HIM

THE FOXES HAVE HOLES
THE BIRDS HAVE NESTS

BUT HE – – A VAGRANT
HE'S IMPOSSIBLE

THEY'LL REDUCE HIM TO SIZE
HE REALLY FANCIES HIMSELF TO BE SOMETHING

SEETHING WITH RAGE
THE DEMONS SWEEP THE WAVES UP

IT'S LIKE THE FLOOD
THE CHAOS AT THE BEGINNING


THE DISCIPLES     IN PANIC
BUT JESUS         HE SLEEPS

THE SLEEP OF THE JUST
COMPLETELY MASTER OF THE SITUATION

OF COURSE IT'S GREAT WHAT HE IS DOING
THEY HAVE THE GREATEST ADMIRATION FOR HIM
BUT HE'S REALLY GOT TO GO

BEFORE IT STARTS TO COST
EVEN MORE

TAKE A LOOK
AT WHERE HE FEELS AT HOME
HE'S A FINE ONE

A FRIEND
OF TAX COLLECTORS AND SINNERS
THEY'RE ON TO THAT

THOSE ARE DISCIPLES
TRY TO SWALLOW ALL OF THAT!

THEY DON'T BELIEVE, DO THEY,
ALL THAT TALK ABOUT THE DOCTOR
WHO NEEDS TO BE WITH THE SICK?

THEY SURE DON'T

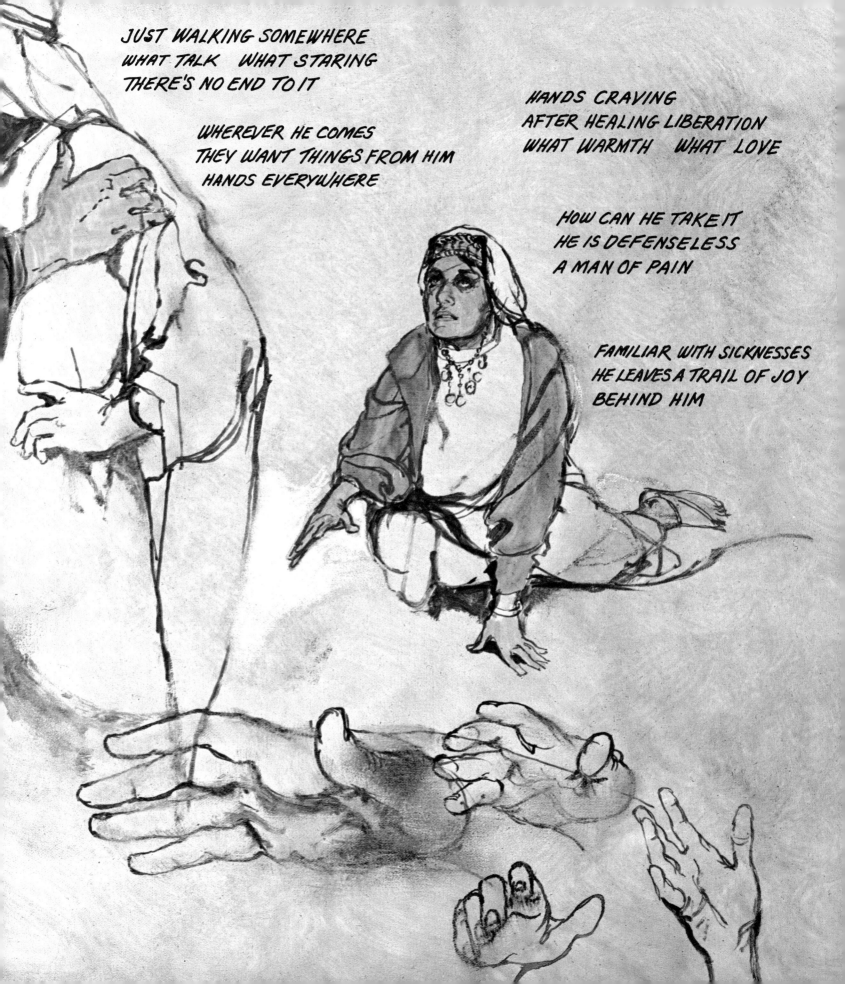

JUST WALKING SOMEWHERE
WHAT TALK   WHAT STARING
THERE'S NO END TO IT

WHEREVER HE COMES
THEY WANT THINGS FROM HIM
HANDS EVERYWHERE

HANDS CRAVING
AFTER HEALING LIBERATION
WHAT WARMTH   WHAT LOVE

HOW CAN HE TAKE IT
HE IS DEFENSELESS
A MAN OF PAIN

FAMILIAR WITH SICKNESSES
HE LEAVES A TRAIL OF JOY
BEHIND HIM

YESTERDAY SHE WAS
PLAYING
LAUGHING
SINGING

THE ONE WHO IS THE MOST SADDENED
IS OF COURSE JESUS

A GIRL LIKE THAT
SHOULDN'T BE DEAD

IT CAN'T BE TRUE
SHE'S SLEEPING
HE'LL TEACH HIS ENEMY THAT

HE SHOULD LEAVE CHILDREN WELL ENOUGH ALONE

HE CALLS HER NAME
TAKES HER HAND

AS IF IT WERE POSSIBLE

AND IT IS

DO THEY KNOW WHAT AWAITS THEM?

THEY'LL DESPAIR
BE MOCKED  HATED  THREATENED  PERSECUTED
THEIR QUIET LIFE IS A THING OF THE PAST

EITHER YOU BELONG TO JESUS OR YOU DON'T

NOW THEY HAVE HIM
HE CAN'T ESCAPE NOW

THE SABBATH-VIOLATOR
THE DESTROYER OF THE LAW

IF THEY DIDN'T REALIZE IT BEFORE
LOOK, HE'S AT IT AGAIN

WHAT IS HE SAYING?
MERCY
HE, LORD OF THE SABBATH?

THAT FINISHES HIM!

HE ALWAYS WAS A BIT STRANGE
BUT THIS TAKES THE CAKE

LISTEN TO HIM--
THE NOTE THAT HE STRIKES WITH THEM
GUARANTEED TO IRRITATE PEOPLE
WHERE DOES HE GET THE RIGHT?

A TOUCH OF MODESTY WOULD HELP HIM
AFTER ALL, WHO DOES HE THINK HE IS?

THE CARPENTER'S SON

JUST SEND THEM HOME,
WITHOUT EATING?

THEY STILL DON'T KNOW HIM

HOW COULD HE --
THEIR FRIEND   THEIR BROTHER
THEIR LIGHT   THEIR BREAD

HE LOVES THEM SO

BUT FIVE LOAVES
   AND TWO FISHES?

ENOUGH
   FOR ONE WHO LOVES

BUT LOOK   JUST TRY IT
   WHOEVER SHARES,
   MULTIPLIES

A BLESSING RESTS UPON IT

HAVING GONE THROUGH SO MUCH WITH HIM, THEY SHOULD HAVE KNOWN BETTER
BUT NO ONE RECOGNIZES HIM, A GHOST -- THEY SCREAM,
JESUS TREMBLES, WHATEVER HE DOES, HE IS AND REMAINS FOR THEM

A STRANGER ——

THAT WOMAN IS BEGINNING TO BE A PAIN
JESUS OUGHT TO DO SOMETHING ABOUT HER

UNPERTURBABLE HE WALKS ON ———————————————————

THE WOMAN WOULDN'T THINK OF GIVING UP
SHE THROWS HERSELF AT HIS FEET

BUT JESUS IS UNYIELDING
BREAD IS FOR THE CHILDREN

BUT THE CRUMBS, SHE ASKS,
AREN'T THEY FOR THE DOGS?

AT THIS JESUS WILL NOT BE OUTDONE
THAT IS WHAT HE CALLS FAITH

THE DISCIPLES COULD USE SOME OF THAT

WHATEVER HE DOES
THEY WILL NOT BELIEVE

THE AIR IS RED
IT TEEMS WITH SIGNS

THE LAME WALK   THE DEAD LIVE
THE POOR RECEIVE THE GOSPEL

HEALING AND RECONCILIATION
ARE NOT FROM OUT OF THE BLUE

THEY SEE IT WITH THEIR OWN EYES
HOW ARE THEY SUPPOSED TO SEE IT

GRADUALLY HE CHANGES BEFORE THEIR VERY EYES
WHO IS HE, IS HE STILL ONE OF THEM ?

FOR A WHILE THEY WILL SEE HIM AS HE IS

A MAN AFTER GOD'S OWN HEART, THE HIGH POINT OF GOD'S JOY
TRUE SON OF HIS FATHER

THEIR EYES WILL NOT BE ABLE TO BEAR IT

A CHILD
LISTENS A WHILE
IS EXPECTANT

THINKS LITTLE OF ITSELF
FINDS IT EASY TO KNEEL

PLAYS A BIT
SINGS

A CHILD
LAUGHS AT ITSELF

THE DISCIPLES
ARE CAUGHT OFF BASE

WOULD THAT CHILD ———

BUT THE CHILD KNOWS
NOTHING

THEY GO ALONG RELUCTANTLY
JUST A MOMENT AGO THEY WERE HAVING SUCH FUN PLAYING

AT FIRST THEY FIND JESUS STRANGE
AND WHY ARE THOSE BIG MEN LOOKING SO ANGRY

BUT JESUS LAUGHS, MAKES A JOKE
AND HOW HE CAN TELL STORIES!

IT'S AS IF THEY KNEW HIM FOR A REAL LONG TIME
A SHAME, THAT HE HAS TO LEAVE SO QUICKLY

THEY FOLLOW HIM WITH THEIR EYES
THEY STILL FEEL HIS HAND ON THEIR HEADS

IT'S IN JOHN'S NAME
    YOU UNDERSTAND

YOU MUSTN'T TAKE IT AMISS

OF COURSE,
THERE'S NO DOUBT POSSIBLE

BUT YOU ARE THE ONE,
    AREN'T YOU ?

YOU'LL BE HAPPY TO SEE
THAT HER TWO SONS
WILL SOON GET A PLACE
OF HONOR

THEY'VE EARNED IT

SHE CAN ASK, AT LEAST

SHE IS, AFTER ALL, THEIR MOTHER

SHE MEANS WELL
OF COURSE, THIS IS HIS CHANCE

AND MARY, HIS MOTHER
WAITED SO LONG

WHAT IS HE UPSET ABOUT?
HE DOESN'T LET HIMSELF BE ORDERED ABOUT

CERTAINLY NOT BY HIS MOTHER

GOT TO SEE HIM
NO MATTER WHAT

HE MAKES HIMSELF
COMPLETELY RIDICULOUS

DOESN'T BELIEVE HIS EARS
HE RUNS HOME

OPEN ARMS
OPEN HEART

ANOTHER PERSON
BEGINS TO LIVE

THE NIGHT IS THE SAFEST
HE MIGHT BE SEEN

A REAL CONVERSATION WOULD BE PREMATURE
NICODEMUS DOESN'T GIVE HIMSELF AWAY
HE HIDES AND DEFENDS HIMSELF

SLOWLY IT BECOMES LIGHT
HE HURRIES
LESS CERTAIN THAN WHEN HE CAME

JESUS' WORDS
WON'T LEAVE HIM ALONE
SEED OF REBIRTH

REBIRTH ?

HE'LL FIND OUT

HE IS DIFFERENT — WHAT DOES HE WANT
SHE DOESN'T LIKE THAT TYPE

SHE DOESN'T LET HERSELF BE KNOWN
MOCKING, SHE STARES AT HIM
DISCUSSION? FINE, SHE GOES ALONG


SHE BECOMES MORE AND MORE UNSURE
HE SEEMS TO KNOW HER


WHO IS HE?

JUST AS HE KNOWS HER

FAILED AGAIN
WILL THEY EVER TRIP HIM UP?

TO CAESAR WHAT BELONGS TO CAESAR
TO GOD WHAT BELONGS TO GOD

OF COURSE, TO EACH HIS OWN
AND GOD IS THE LORD

THEY WON'T BE SECOND BEST IN THAT
ASHAMED THEY SLINK AWAY

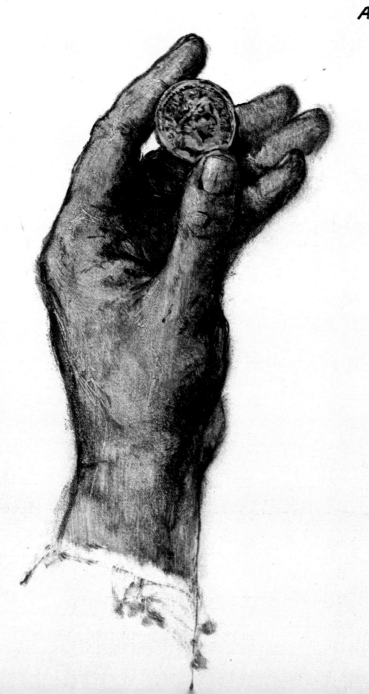

SHE GIVES IT
WITH ALL HER HEART

IT ISN'T MUCH

IT WEIGHS A LOT FOR GOD


SHE GIVES HERSELF

LIKE BOOTY
THEY DRAG HER ALONG
TRIUMPHANT

CAUGHT IN THE ACT
SHE SHOULD BE STONED
OR DOES HE THINK NOT ?

DEFIANTLY THEY LOOK AT HIM
SOURED WOMEN
STAND THERE CHUCKLING

HOW HE SETS THEM BACK ON THEIR HEELS
THE HYPOCRITES

OF COURSE HE'S FAITHFUL
TO THE LAW OF MOSES
WHAT DO THEY THINK ?

BUT JUST FOR THAT REASON

JUST LET THEM THROW
THE FIRST STONE

IF THEY DARE

SHE DOESN'T KNOW WHY
BUT IT HAS TO BE
THERE'S STILL TIME

JESUS UNDERSTANDS

HE NEEDED THIS
IT WILL BE COLD
AND QUIET ENOUGH

THE DISCIPLES   CONFRONT A RIDDLE

JUDAS
KNOWS WHAT  HE IS UP TO

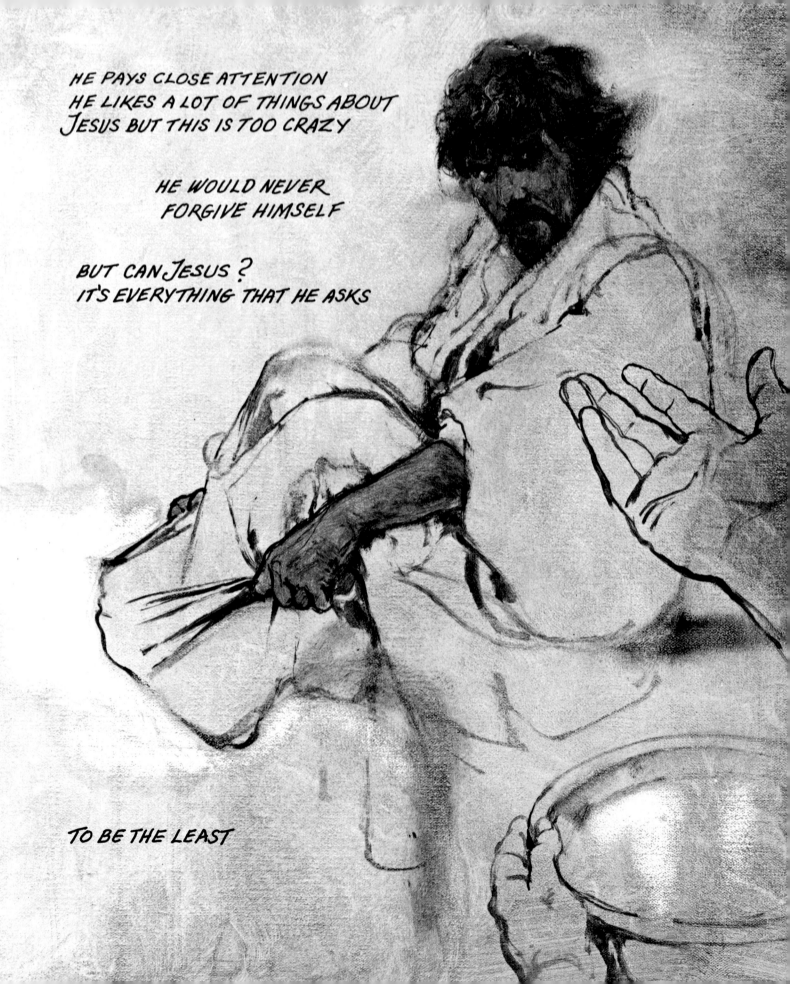

HE PAYS CLOSE ATTENTION
HE LIKES A LOT OF THINGS ABOUT
JESUS BUT THIS IS TOO CRAZY

HE WOULD NEVER
FORGIVE HIMSELF

BUT CAN JESUS?
IT'S EVERYTHING THAT HE ASKS

TO BE THE LEAST

HIS DECISION IS SET
HE CAN NO LONGER TURN BACK

EVEN IF HE WANTED TO

AT THE CRITICAL MOMENT
HE MEETS HIS HOUR ALONE
THAT IS CLEAR


EVEN HIS BEST FRIENDS
ARE NO LONGER UP TO IT

EVEN PETER
HE CAN'T COUNT ON


ALL ALONE


THE WORST IS STILL TO COME

WHY A KISS, NOW?

MORE DEADLY THAN OUTRIGHT
HOSTILITY IS PRETENDED FRIENDSHIP

FRIENDSHIP WHICH ONCE WAS GENUINE

AS IF HE COULDN'T GIVE OUT A CHEER
FINALLY--THE CASE IS COMING TO A CLOSE


BUT HE CONTAINS HIMSELF

FRIEND
BROTHER
HOPE
SALVATION
RESURRECTION
LIFE

BUT HE MUST DIE

CONFESSED HIM AS NO OTHER
PROMISED HIM ARDENT FIDELITY
AND HE MEANT IT

THAT'S HOW HE IS

IF WORST COMES TO WORST
GIVE THE IMPRESSION HE HAD NOTHING
TO DO WITH HIM -- DOESN'T KNOW THE MAN

WHILE HE LOVES HIM SO MUCH

IT'S THEIR PROBLEM
THEY HAVE JESUS
AND THAT'S WHAT IT WAS ALL ABOUT

JUDAS MUST BE ABLE TO SEE
WHAT WILL COME OF IT
HE KNEW WHAT HE WAS DOING,
                    DIDN'T HE?


HE KNEW

HE SITS THERE
THOSE ACCURSED JEWS TOO

O. K., THEY'LL GET THEIR WAY
JESUS MAY BE INNOCENT
HIS REST IS ALSO WORTH SOMETHING
TO HIM

IF HIS WIFE HAD ONLY
NOT PESTERED HIM WITH THAT
DREAM

A FINE KING
TO HAVE SPORT WITH

HE'S GETTING WHAT IS COMING
                         TO HIM
IT WON'T BE THEIR FAULT

   AS THOUGH HE WAS MADE OF STONE

THEY'LL HAVE THEIR WAY WITH HIM
HE HAS ONLY HIMSELF TO BLAME

NOW WHY HIM, A MERE PASSERBY?
IT WILL COME OUT BAD FOR HIM ——
HE'D BETTER GET A MOVE ON

HE SEES THAT HE'D BETTER OBEY
RELUCTANTLY HE TAKES THE CROSS UPON HIMSELF

IT'LL LEAVE ITS MARK ON HIM
GRADUALLY HE'LL BECOME A FOLLOWER OF JESUS

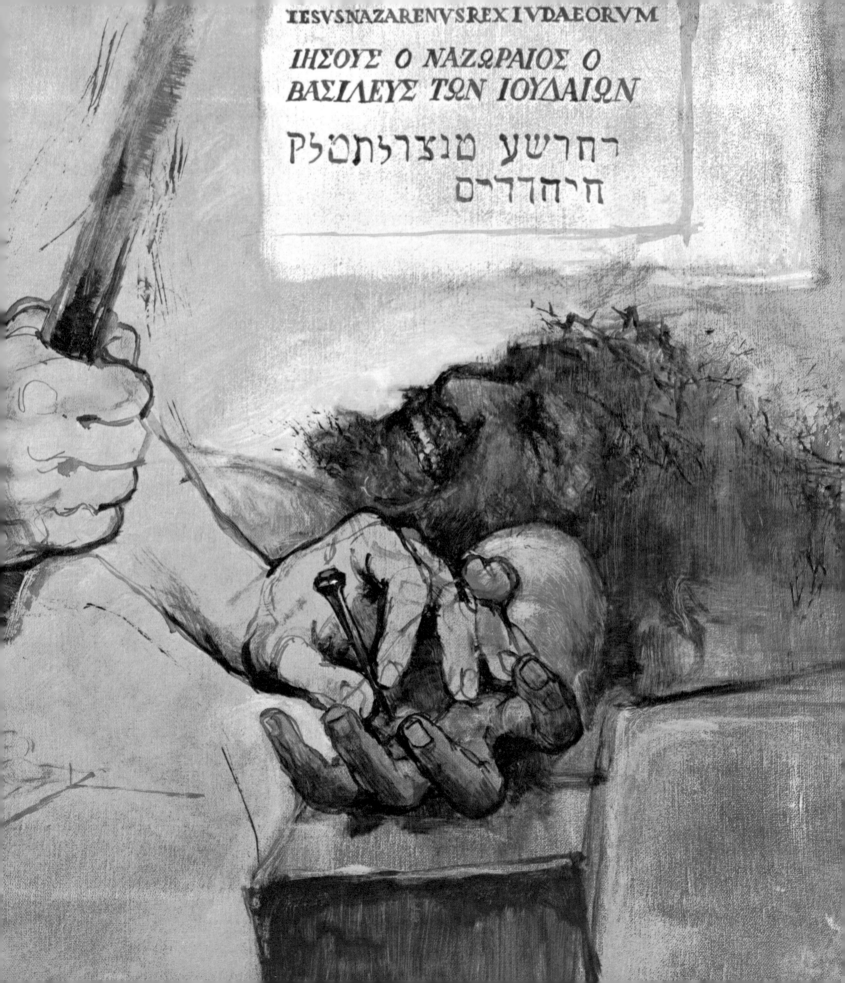

IT'S NOT JUST A MATTER OF HANGING
THIS IS TOUGH WORK!

TO THE VERY END
HE REMAINS REACHABLE

A FRIEND   A BROTHER
A RESCUER IN NEED

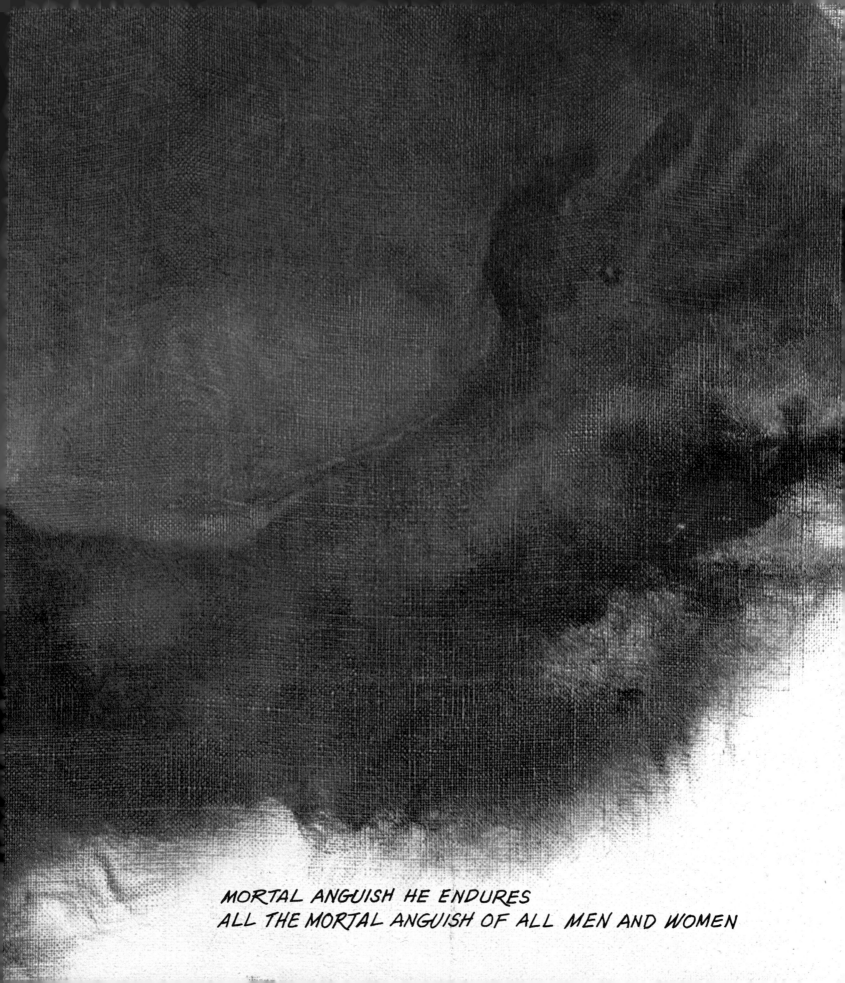

MORTAL ANGUISH HE ENDURES
ALL THE MORTAL ANGUISH OF ALL MEN AND WOMEN

WHAT HE HAS SEEN
NO ONE HAS SEEN
NO ONE SHALL SEE AGAIN

HE'S FINISHED
HE MUST BE TAKEN AWAY

NEVER AGAIN THAT VOICE
NEVER AGAIN THAT LOOK

THEY WILL HAVE TO GO ON
WITHOUT HIM

THE ONLY THING
LEFT FOR THEM

IS TO BURY HIM
           THE FINAL HONOR

what they've just
gone through

IF THEY'D ONLY KEEP
THEIR MOUTHS SHUT

HIS DISCIPLES
HAVE STOLEN HIM
AND THAT'S THAT

OR DO THEY WANT
EVEN MORE MONEY?

SHE LIVES IN ANOTHER WORLD

DEAD IS DEAD
EVERYTHING ENDS

the way he called her by name
It's Jesus he's alive!
She's afire with joy
THE FLAMES BURST OUT OF HER
SHE STARTS LIVING, AT LAST

WHO HAD COUNTED ON SOMETHING LIKE THIS?
THEY HAD ALREADY RESIGNED THEMSELVES TO IT

UNBELIEVABLE--BUT THEY STILL NEED TO
CHECK THOSE HANDS AND THAT SIDE

SLOWLY THEIR HEARTS OPEN UP

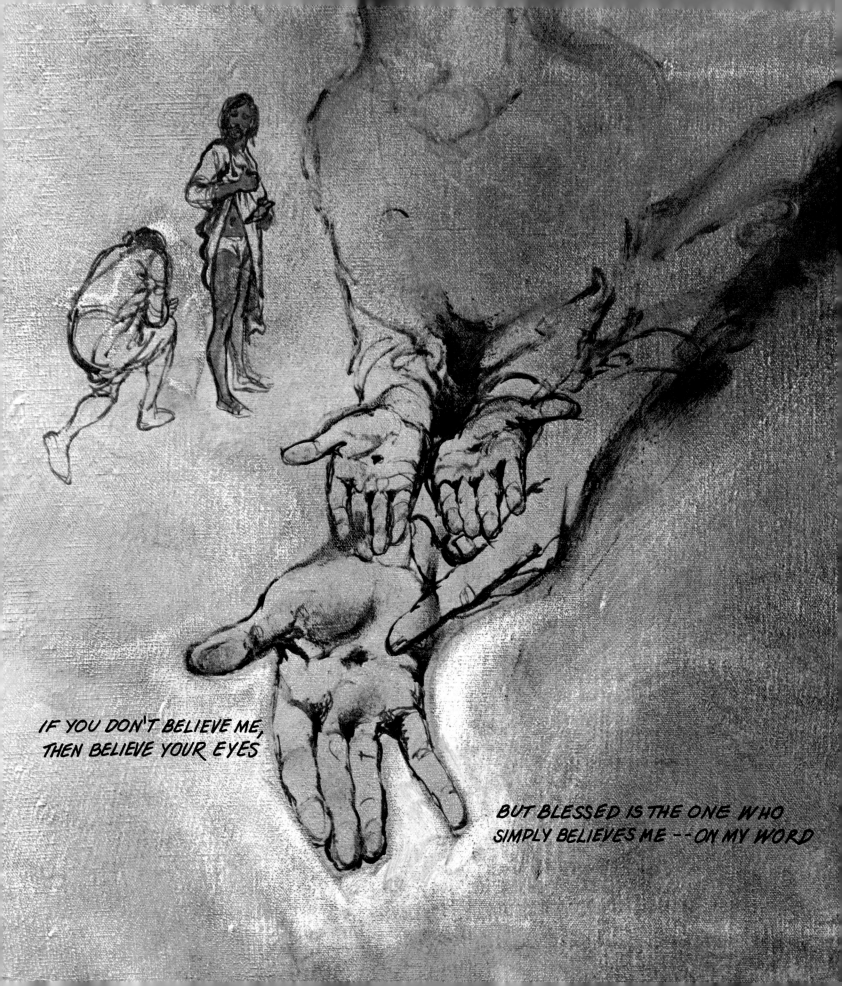

IF YOU DON'T BELIEVE ME,
THEN BELIEVE YOUR EYES

BUT BLESSED IS THE ONE WHO
SIMPLY BELIEVES ME --ON MY WORD

NOW IT ALL DEPENDS ON THEM
Jesus ENTRUSTS EVERYTHING TO THEM

WILL THEY CONTINUE HIS WORK?
WILL THEY LIVE IN HIS SPIRIT?

THAT SPIRIT WILL BE WITH THEM

# Contents